ANACONDA

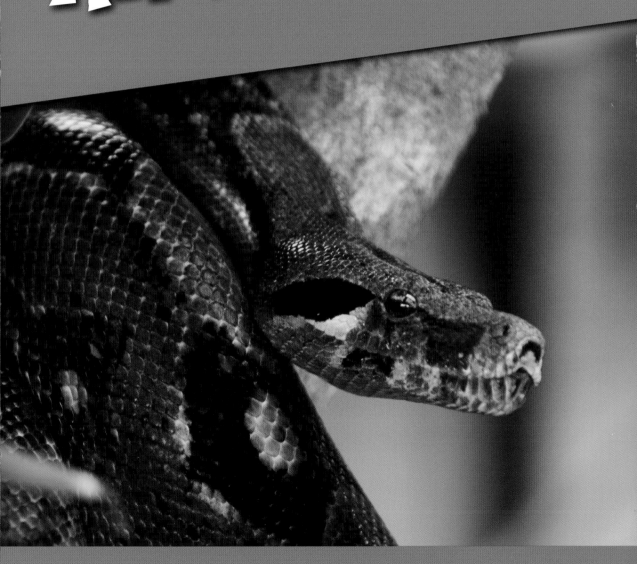

SAMANTHA BELL

Published in the United States of America by Cherry Lake Publishing
Ann Arbor, Michigan
www.cherrylakepublishing.com

Content Adviser: Dr. Stephen S. Ditchkoff, Professor of Wildlife Ecology, Auburn University, Alabama
Reading Adviser: Marla Conn, ReadAbility, Inc.

Photo Credits: ©Martin Krause/Thinkstock, cover, 1; ©Tom Brakefield/Thinkstock, 5; ©Red List Index (Sampled Approach), Zoological Society London 2010, 6; ©Phil Whitehouse/http://www.flickr.com/CC-BY-2.0, 7; ©Patrick K. Campbell/Shutterstock Images, 8, 21; ©JoeFotoSS/Shutterstock Images, 11; ©Dorling Kindersley/Thinkstock, 12; ©FOTOMIRO/Shutterstock Images, 14; ©ATesevich/Shutterstock Images, 15; ©chameleunejai/Shutterstock Images, 17, 20; ©Melinda Millward, 19; ©Dr. Morley Read/Shutterstock Images, 23; ©Robin Winkelman/Dreamstime.com, 25; ©milosk50/Shutterstock Images, 27; ©Fernando Flores/http://www.flickr.com/CC-BY-SA 2.0, 28

Library of Congress Cataloging-in-Publication Data

Bell, Samantha, author.
Anaconda / by Samantha Bell.
     pages cm. -— (Exploring our rainforests)
     Summary: "Introduces facts about anacondas, including physical features, habitat, life cycle, food, and threats to these rainforest creatures. Photos, captions, and keywords supplement the narrative of this informational text."
— Provided by publisher.
     Audience: Ages 8-12.
     Audience: Grades 4 to 6.
     ISBN 978-1-63188-973-8 (hardcover) — ISBN 978-1-63362-012-4 (pbk.) —
     ISBN 978-1-63362-051-3 (pdf) — ISBN 978-1-63362-090-2 (ebook) 1. Anaconda—Juvenile literature. I. Title.

QL666.O63B45 2014
597.96'7—dc23   2014020994

Cherry Lake Publishing would like to acknowledge the work of
The Partnership for 21st Century Skills. Please visit www.p21.org
for more information.

Printed in the United States of America
Corporate Graphics

ABOUT THE AUTHOR

Samantha Bell lives in South Carolina with her husband, four children, and lots of animals. She has written and/or illustrated more than 20 books for children. She loves being outdoors and learning about all the amazing wonders of nature.

TABLE OF CONTENTS

A SSSSECRETIVE SNAKE

A slow-moving stream winds its way through a tropical rainforest in South America. A toucan calls from overhead. **Capybaras** play around the bank. The scene may look peaceful, but moving silently through the water is one of the world's largest snakes, the green anaconda.

Green anacondas are just slightly shorter than their cousins, the reticulated python. But their bodies are so big around that they are almost twice as heavy. Three smaller **species** of anacondas also inhabit the

[21ST CENTURY SKILLS LIBRARY]

Anacondas are skilled at swimming.

rainforests. The smaller species include the yellow anaconda, the dark-spotted anaconda, and the Bolivian anaconda. As members of the boa family, these anacondas are **constrictors**. To kill their prey, such as a capybara, they wrap themselves around it, cutting off its air supply.

Because of their bulky size and weight, anacondas move more smoothly through the water than on land. Many are found near rivers, streams, lakes, ponds, swamps, and even ditches. Anacondas that live near water stay active all throughout the year.

RANGE MAP

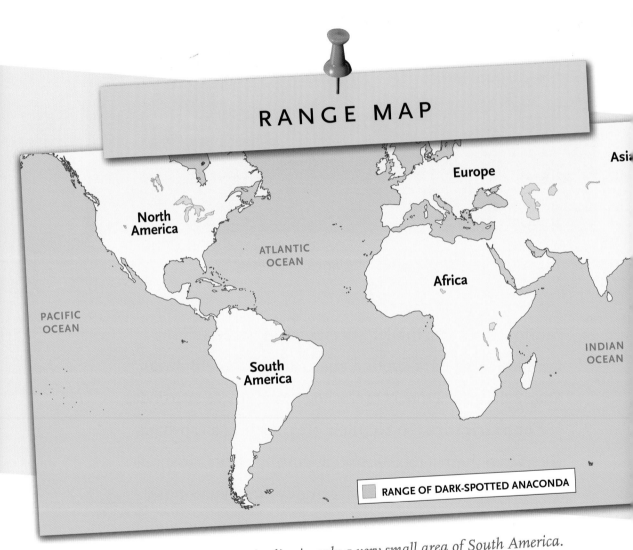

North America

ATLANTIC OCEAN

Europe

Asia

Africa

PACIFIC OCEAN

South America

INDIAN OCEAN

■ RANGE OF DARK-SPOTTED ANACONDA

Dark-spotted anacondas live in only a very small area of South America.

[21ST CENTURY SKILLS LIBRARY]

Anacondas burrow holes in the mud, where they can hide themselves.

Anacondas can also be found in dry forests, **savannas**, and treeless prairies called *llanos*. During the rainy season, these areas flood and stay covered with water for 6 to 8 months each year. The anacondas swim and hunt in the water. During the dry months, the snakes look for shelter. They bury themselves in mud or hide in caves under tree roots near the riverbank.

Anacondas have a distinctive skin pattern.

Anacondas are found throughout South America. Green anacondas are common in the northern countries, in the tropical rainforests of the Orinoco and Amazon **river basins**. They are also found on the island of Trinidad. Yellow anacondas live in the southern part of South America in Paraguay, southern Brazil, Bolivia, and Argentina. Dark-spotted anacondas are found in French Guiana and northern Brazil. Bolivian anacondas, which live in northeastern Bolivia, were discovered in 2002.

[21ST CENTURY SKILLS LIBRARY]

Like other snakes, the anaconda is cold-blooded. It's able to regulate its body temperature with heat from the sun, however. Anacondas warm themselves along riverbanks or in tree branches that hang over the water. If they need to cool down, they move into the shade. If they are threatened, they can drop quickly into the water.

Anacondas are **solitary** animals. Each one usually stays in the same habitat all its life, rarely moving out of its **home range**. But anacondas are very secretive. The color and patterns of their skin help camouflage them in the mud and muck, as well as among plants floating in the water. Because they can be so hard to find, scientists still have much to learn about them.

THINK ABOUT IT

IF ANACONDAS ARE SUCH LARGE SNAKES, WHY DO YOU THINK IT TOOK SO LONG FOR SCIENTISTS TO DISCOVER THE BOLIVIAN ANACONDA?

SNAKE SENSES

Over the years, reports from the rainforests told of giant anacondas living there. While they were probably exaggerations, some scientists believe that such animals just might exist deep in the forests. It's easy to see why. Green anacondas can grow from 20 to 32 feet (6 to 9.7 meters) long—as long as a school bus! As one of the world's heaviest snakes, a green anaconda can weigh up to 550 pounds (249.5 kilograms). One of the largest anacondas ever caught measured 44 inches (111.8 centimeters) around. That's bigger around than a basketball!

[21ST CENTURY SKILLS LIBRARY]

Yellow anacondas are much smaller. Adults usually measure between 10 and 13 feet (3 to 4 m) long. Dark-spotted anacondas are roughly the same size. The longest Bolivian anaconda ever found was 10.5 feet (3.2 m) long. In each species, the female snakes are longer than the males and weigh more.

Female anacondas are bigger than the males.

BODY DIAGRAM

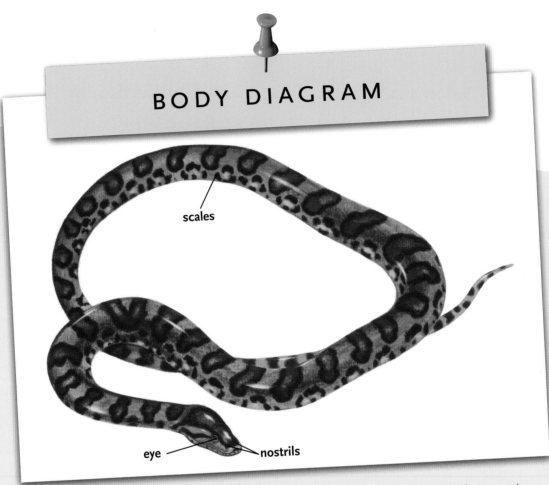

scales

eye — nostrils

Anacondas have dark-colored scales to help them blend in with their environment.

All anacondas blend in with the murky water or vegetation of their surroundings. Green anacondas are usually brownish-green, grayish-green, or olive green. This color gradually changes to yellow on the **ventral** side. Small, smooth scales cover their bodies. The yellow anaconda has yellowish-green or yellowish-tan scales with brown or black blotches on its back and sides. The Bolivian anaconda looks very similar to the yellow anaconda. The dark-spotted anaconda is brown with large dark spots.

The anacondas' bodies, not just their skin, are also well-suited for the snakes' watery habitat. Anacondas are excellent swimmers and divers and move effortlessly through the water. Their eyes and nostrils are on the tops of their heads, which lets them watch for prey while the rest of their bodies are hidden underwater.

Anacondas may not have sharp eyesight, but they have other ways of finding their prey. Specialized sensory organs along their lips sense heat from warm-blooded animals. This helps them find nearby prey even in the dark. Anacondas can also detect sounds, even though they don't have an **external** ear. They "hear" sounds and vibrations through their sensitive skin. They can detect movement both on the ground and through the water.

Anacondas use their tongues to "smell" the air.

Like all snakes, anacondas have a flicking forked tongue. But the tongue isn't for tasting. Instead, it collects chemical signals from the air, then brings those signals back in to the roof of the snake's mouth. There, a sensory organ called the Jacobson's organ reads the signals. If potential prey is nearby, the anaconda will know.

This fierce snake was created in a sand sculpture competition.

LOOK AGAIN

LOOK AT THIS SAND SCULPTURE OF AN ANACONDA. WHICH BODY PARTS LOOK THE SAME AS ON A LIVE ONE? WHICH PARTS ARE DIFFERENT?

Hold On Tight

Anacondas are **carnivores**, hunting a variety of animals. **Juvenile** snakes feed on smaller prey such as young **caimans** and small birds. When they grow older, they will also eat fish, turtles, birds, lizards, wild pigs, anteaters, and capybaras. They will even eat deer, jaguars, and grown caimans! Sometimes the larger female anacondas will eat the males.

Anacondas don't chase their prey. Instead, they watch and wait for the animal to swim by or come to the water to drink. The color and patterns of the anacondas' skin

Anacondas have long tongues, which they use for smelling prey.

help hide them until it's time to strike. Anacondas are opportunistic predators, eating any prey they can kill and swallow.

An anaconda will attack any time of the day. When the snake senses another animal, it waits until the prey comes close enough. Then the anaconda bites the animal with more than 100 pointed teeth, which prevent the prey from pulling free and escaping. Anacondas aren't **venomous**. Instead, they use their teeth for grabbing and holding the prey.

As the anaconda bites the prey, the snake wraps its body all around the animal. The harder the animal struggles, the tighter the snake coils. Then the snake squeezes the animal until it can't breathe or until the circulation of its blood is cut off. Sometimes the anaconda pulls the animal underwater and drowns it.

When the animal is dead, the snake slowly relaxes its coils. But it doesn't chew up its prey. Its mouth can open wide enough to swallow the animal whole. The snake's skull bones are loosely held together by stretchy **ligaments**. The lower jaw isn't connected to the upper jaw. The skin around the mouth is very thick, and can stretch around the whole body of the prey.

The anaconda swallows its prey headfirst. Sometimes the snake will take its meal underwater. Scientists believe the water helps the snake move the food into the right position for swallowing. If an anaconda is disturbed as it's eating, it will coil around the prey and try to drag it away. The anaconda won't let go, even if it is attacked.

Anacondas need to rest after eating a huge meal.

Because anacondas eat very large animals, their jaws need to open wide.

After a big meal, anacondas can go for weeks or even months without eating again.

Green anacondas are one of the few snakes large enough to eat humans. There aren't any proven cases of anacondas swallowing people, however. Anaconda attacks are actually very rare, probably because few people live in the same areas as the snakes. When people have been bitten, it might have been because the snake was defending itself. Other times, the snake might have mistaken the person for prey.

Anacondas often spend their time in rivers.

LOOK AGAIN

ANACONDAS HAVE PATTERNS THAT HELP THEM HIDE WITHIN THEIR SURROUNDINGS. CAN YOU THINK OF OTHER PREDATORS THAT USE CAMOUFLAGE IN THEIR HUNT FOR PREY?

Baby Bonanza!

Anacondas are ready to mate when they are about 3 to 4 years old. They mate during the rainforest's dry season between March and May. During this time, females don't move around much. They can often be seen **basking** on the riverbanks. Males travel from all directions to find females to mate with. They constantly test the air with their tongues to pick up the female's scent. If two males come across each other, they may fight, but fighting is rare. If one male is very large, it may be mistaken by another as a female. The other male may try to court it.

This anaconda is a young one—a juvenile.

When males do find a female, they will compete for her. They surround the female, forming a twisting, writhing ball. During that time, the females will choose which male or males they prefer, and they will mate with one or more of them. After mating, the female may eat one of the males. She won't eat again until after the babies are born. The other males leave the female and return to their home range.

Anacondas don't lay eggs. Instead, the young form inside the mother's body. This helps protect them from predators. They are attached to a yolk sac and surrounded by a clear membrane instead of a shell.

Inside the mother, the babies are kept at a fairly constant temperature. As with other reptiles, temperatures affect how fast the young grow. Anacondas will often bask in the sun to raise their body temperatures, which will make the babies grow faster.

After 6 to 7 months, the female gives birth to 20 to 100 live babies. The young are still surrounded by the protective membrane, so they must break it open. Baby green anacondas are about 2 feet (0.6 m) long when born. Almost immediately, they are able to swim and hunt. They hide to protect themselves from predators. They are completely on their own from birth—their mother doesn't take care of them at all. She will mate again in another year.

Anacondas live about 10 years in the wild. In captivity they can live to be 20 or even 30 years old.

Once the female anaconda is old enough, she will mate every year.

LOOK AGAIN

Look at this female anaconda. How do you think she will protect her young?

AMAZON APPETITES

Although anacondas can capture large prey, they themselves are sometimes the prey. Larger caimans and jaguars catch and eat the juveniles and small adult snakes. To avoid a predator, green anacondas will either hide by burrowing in the mud or escaping into nearby water. If directly threatened or attacked, the anaconda will coil up into a ball and strike at the attacker. Smaller anacondas have been known to be very aggressive and to bite frequently. The snakes also defend themselves by letting out a bad smell.

Jaguars are sometimes able to catch and eat anacondas.

Anacondas are a big part of South American culture.

Anacondas are at risk when they are feeding. The anaconda will not let go of its prey, even if it is being attacked itself. Once it is done eating, the snake weighs a lot more, and can't move very well on land.

Humans are the biggest threat to anacondas. People catch the snakes to eat them. Anacondas are an excellent source of protein, and their large size provides a lot of food. The people of Brazil and Peru also use the green anacondas as medicine for health problems such as infections and asthma. Some believe the snakes have magical and spiritual qualities, and their body parts are sold for religious ceremonies.

People also hunt anacondas for their skin. The anacondas' skin is turned into leather and made into shoes, purses, and belts. Some anacondas are taken and sold as pets.

Human activity also threatens the anacondas' habitat. Some jungles are being destroyed as the trees are cut down. But field studies of the anacondas continue to provide new information about them. The more we know, the better we will be able to protect and appreciate these giants of the Amazon.

GO DEEPER

Grown anacondas eat leopards, and leopards eat young anacondas. Can you think of other animals that are both the predator and the prey?

THINK ABOUT IT

- The Bolivian anaconda was recently discovered, and very little is known about its behavior. From what you know about other anacondas, what can you assume is true about the Bolivian anaconda? What might be different?

- Anacondas have been depicted as man-eaters in scary movies and books. From what you've learned about anacondas, is that an accurate portrayal? Give examples to support your answer.

- Anacondas are sometimes caught and sold as pets. Do you think they make good pets? Why or why not?

- Find a video on the Internet that features anacondas. How is the video's information the same or different from what you've read in this book?

LEARN MORE

FURTHER READING

Fredericks, Anthony D. *A is for Anaconda: A Rainforest Alphabet*. Ann Arbor, MI: Sleeping Bear Press, 2013.

Mattern, Joanne. *Anacondas*. Mankato, MN: Capstone Press, 2009.

Taylor, Barbara. *Animal Giants*. Boston: Kingfisher, 2004.

WEB SITES

Bronx Zoo—Anaconda
www.bronxzoo.com/animals-and-exhibits/animals/reptiles-and-amphibians/anaconda.aspx
Read more facts about anacondas and find out why they are hunted illegally.

National Geographic—Anaconda Hunts
http://video.nationalgeographic.com/video/anaconda_stalkscapybara
Watch this exciting video of an anaconda on the hunt for food.

National Geographic Kids—Anaconda
http://kids.nationalgeographic.com/kids/animals/creaturefeature/anaconda/
View up-close photos of an anaconda and read a little about it.

GLOSSARY

basking (BASK-ing) lying or relaxing in a pleasant, warm atmosphere

caimans (KEYH-muhnz) reptiles resembling alligators

capybaras (kap-uh-BAHR-uhz) tailless South American rodents that grow to be about 4 feet (1.2 m) long

carnivores (KAHR-nuh-vorz) animals that eat other animals

constrictors (kuhn-STRIK-terz) snakes that kill their prey by coiling around it and squeezing it

external (ek-STUR-nuhl) on the outside of something

home range (hohm reynj) the area in which an animal normally lives

juvenile (JOO-vuh-nuhl) young

ligaments (LIG-uh-muhnts) tough bands of tissue that hold bones together

river basins (RIV-ur BAY-suhnz) the lands that waters flow across on their way to rivers

savannas (suh-VAN-uhz) grasslands containing scattered trees

solitary (SAH-li-ter-ee) all alone

species (SPEE-sheez) particular kinds or types of living things

venomous (VEN-uhm-uss) having the ability to inflict a poisonous wound

ventral (VEN-truhl) the underside or belly

INDEX

[21ST CENTURY SKILLS LIBRARY]